Snapcat

The cats that love to snap (and chat)

ROSIE RYDER

summersdale

SNAPCAT

Summersdale Publishers Ltd
46 West Street
Chichester
West Sussex
PO19 1RP
UK

www.summersdale.com

Printed and bound in China

ISBN: 978-1-78685-195-6

Substantial discounts on bulk quantities of Summersdale books are available to corporations, professional associations and other organisations. For details contact general enquiries: telephone: +44 (0) 1243 771107, fax: +44 (0) 1243 786300 or email: enquiries@summersdale.com.

Disclaimer
This book is not endorsed by, promoted by or associated with Snapchat™.

Meet the snapcats

So, you thought it was only humans who were hooked on Snapchat? Well, think again – we have evidence to the contrary. These are the cats that live in the moment, snapping the world around them and sharing their stories with their feline friends.

These cool kitties have a lot to say, and whether it's with a cheeky sticker or a sassy caption, they say it with style. Find out what they get up to when we're not looking, discover what they're really thinking and prepare to see your fur-miliar friends through a whole new lens…

Looks like someone's had a rough day

Float
like a 🦋
sting like a
🐝

dat ass tho

Selfie Queen #nofilter

#proteingoals

So busted 😄

It's bathtime

Heard u were talkin trash

Shame on you,
Mittens

Help i have fallen

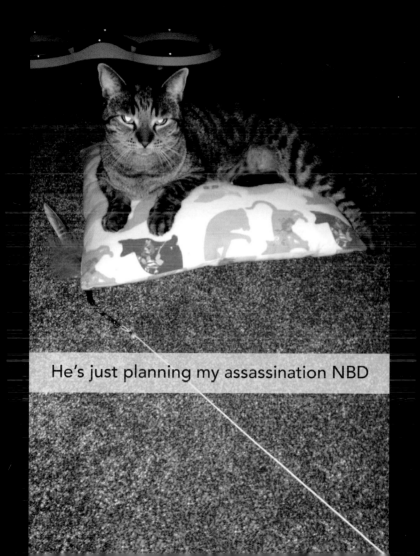

He's just planning my assassination NBD

We accept the presents
we think we deserve

When u know u should do something
useful but u could also sit and do nothing

That's one
Jason Bourne
MF

When ur done adulting for the day

When he tells u to smile

The truth is out there

Someone ate his snacks again

She thinks she's people

Sweet air guitar solo

When u accidentally open
the front-facing camera

Sunshine

**MEATY DINNER
DOG FOOD**

24 LARGE

1568

i do what i want susan

I sense a disturbance in the force

CAN U NOT

When the alarm clock says morning
but u still feel like last night

Nora, cancel my
2 o'clock

TFW ur 500% done with clean eating

🔥 #slay 🔥

Someone just offered him a chicken nugget 🍗

They're ironic

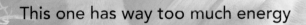

This one has way too much energy

Aw yiss

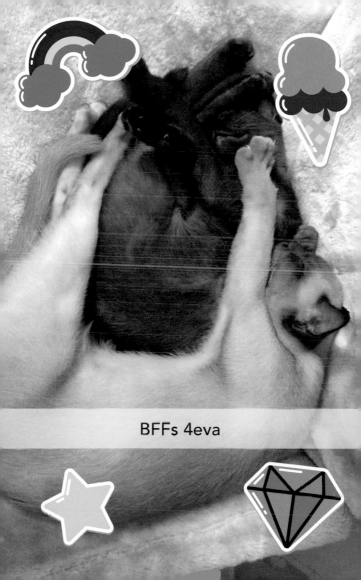

BFFs 4eva

Bae caught me slippin

She's sexy an she know it

Wen u try ur best but u dont succeed

This could be us
but u playin

She knows it's the vet

One day he's gonna turn on us all.

1st January 😖

The risk I took was calculated but man am I bad at maths

Spidey sense is tingling

ladies

Bueno

Snap me like one of ur French girls

o shoot

Twerking...

Just look at this creeper

If I fits,
I sits

Hi this is tom I stole meg's phone lol

When u know he's seen ur message but hasn't replied

Chins 4 dayz

u ok hun?

Wouldn't mess with this one if I were you

#foodbaby

He's plotting something shady I know it.

Problems = 99

Majestic AF.

Hello, this is cat

Soon...

Looks like Marvin's gonna need fixing again

Life is hard.

The Creation of Cat

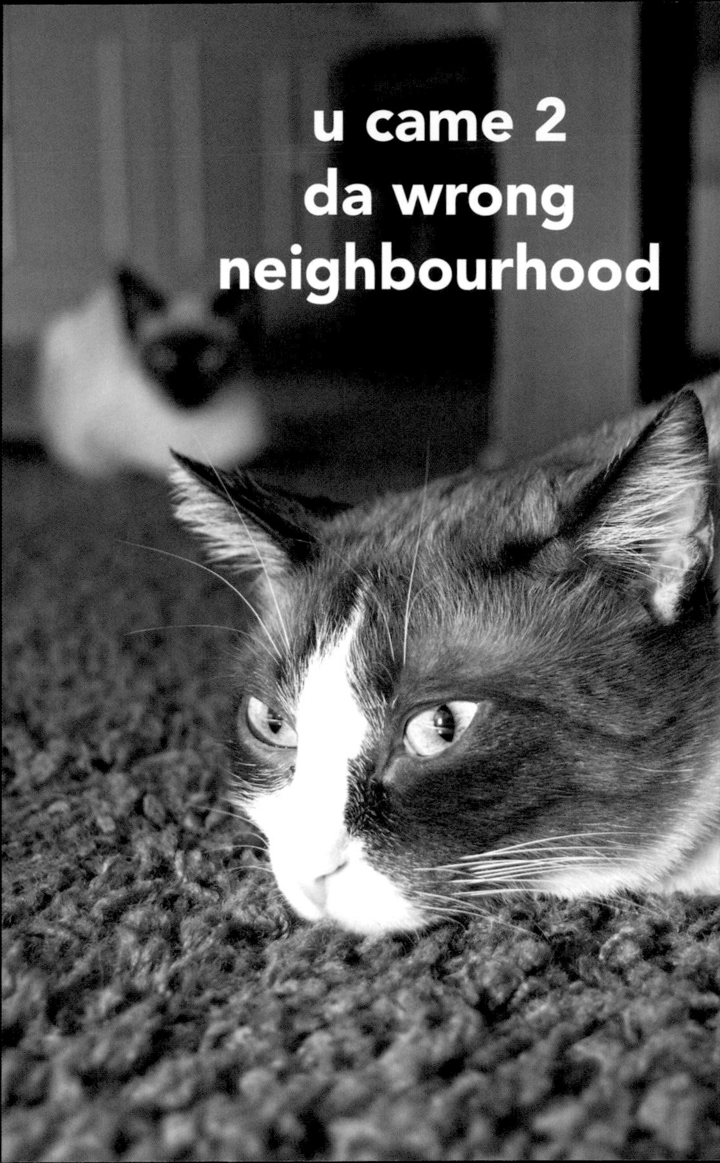
u came 2
da wrong
neighbourhood

When u hear the bath water runnin

#floof

Barbara do u mind?

Waddup

Spoopy

Anyway, here's Wonderwall

Suck it,
Schrödinger.

Party don't start till I walk in

Pretty sure someone's plotting my death

She loved
me once...

i woke up
like dis

Get in loser we're going shopping

my precious

#relationshipgoals

Waiting for tinderella

#hygge

When ur parents have guests round and u just want something from the kitchen.

I have the best hair. It's terrific.
Everyone agrees.

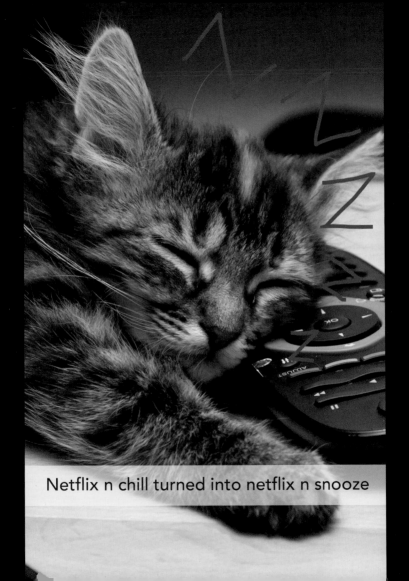

Netflix n chill turned into netflix n snooze

This seat is taken 🚫

What a poser

Trying to get through the week like...

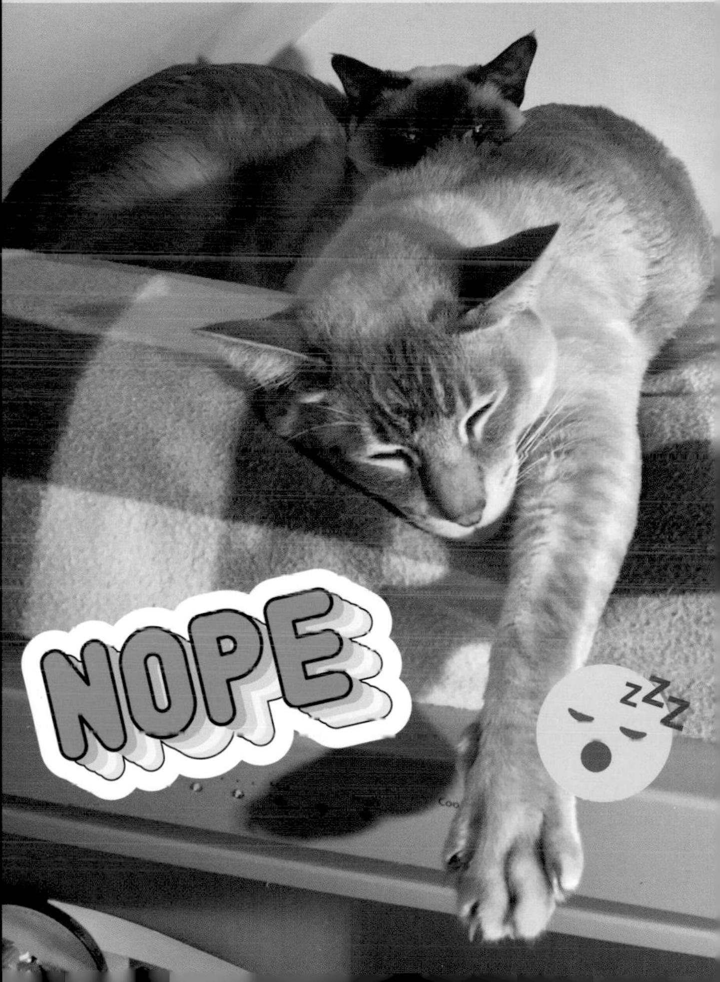

I read *The Girl on the Train*
before it was cool

Carbs is love

Slidin into ur snaps like

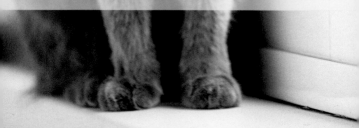
All around me are familiar faces...

Houston she has seen the treats

u kids keep it down ok

Boop

Thug life chose me

When ur mom gets u ready
for the first day of school

Tell me about ur childhood

So close yet so far

Okay get a room guys

Fierce but cute

Send help

Bae 1,
personal space 0

Yaaaaaaassss!

Photo Credits

If you're interested in finding out
more about our books, find us on Facebook
at **Summersdale Publishers** and follow
us on Twitter at **@Summersdale**.

www.summersdale.com